This book belongs to:

____

Made in the USA
Monee, IL
30 November 2019

17719708R00066